DEEP SEA

Mary-Jane Wilkins

W

FRANKLIN WATTS

LONDON•SYDNEY

Franklin Watts
First published in Great Britain in 2016 by
The Watts Publishing Group

For Brown Bear Books Ltd:
Picture Researcher: Clare Newman
Designer: Melissa Roskell
Design Manager: Keith Davis
Editorial Director: Lindsey Lowe
Children's Publisher: Anne O'Daly

ISBN 978 1 4451 5174 8

Printed in China

Franklin Watts
An imprint of
Hachette Children's Group
Part of The Watts Publishing Group
Carmelite House
50 Victoria Embankment
London EC4Y 0DZ

An Hachette UK company
www.hachette.co.uk

www.franklinwatts.co.uk

Picture Credits

The photographs in this book are used by permission and through the courtesy of:

Front Cover: NOAA: cl; Shutterstock: tl, Willyam Bradberry main, Ethan Daniels bl, Richard Whitcombe br;
Inside: 1, ©Shutterstock/Super Joseph; 4, ©NOAA; 4-5, ©Shutterstock/Willyam Bradberry; 6, ©FLPA/Norbert Wu/Minden Pictures; 6-7, ©Shutterstock/Super Joseph; 8, ©Getty Images/Bill Curtsinger/National Geographic; 8-9, ©Photoshot/Paula de Oliveira/NHPA; 10, ©Nature PL/David Shale; 10-11, ©Nature PL/David Shale; 12, ©Nature PL/David Shale; 13, ©Shutterstock/Ethan Daniels; 14, ©Shutterstock/Eric Isselee; 14-15, ©FLPA/Reinhard Dirscherl; 16, ©Corbis/National Geographic Creative; 16-17, ©FLPA/Norbert Wu/Minden Pictures; 18, ©Corbis/Thomas P. Peschak/National Geographic; 18-19, ©Shutterstock/Andreas Fenkie; 20, ©NOAA; 21, ©FLPA/Photo Researchers; 22, ©Shutterstock/Super Joseph; 23, ©Shutterstock/Stefan Pircher.
T=Top, C=Centre, B=Bottom, L=Left, R=Right

Brown Bear Books has made every attempt to contact the copyright holder. If you have any information please contact: licensing@brownbearbooks.co.uk

CONTENTS

Where is the DEEPEST SEA?

Near land, the sea is shallow. About 65 km from shore, the ocean gets deeper. The deepest parts are trenches, and the deepest trench is in the Pacific Ocean.

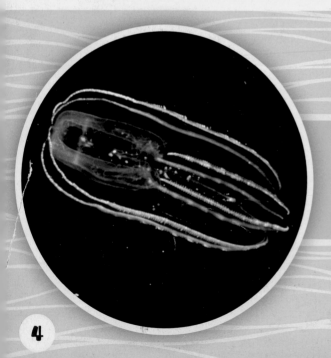

Some animals in the deep, dark sea make their own light.

WOW!

Sea covers nearly three-quarters of the Earth. There are five oceans. The Pacific Ocean is the **biggest**.

Arctic Ocean

Atlantic Ocean

Pacific Ocean

Indian Ocean

Southern Ocean

The deeper you go in the ocean, the darker it gets. It is completely dark below 1,000 m. You can read about some deep-sea animals in this book.

ANGLERFISH

Anglerfish live in the deep sea. A female anglerfish has a **huge** head. A spine pokes out of the top of it. The end of the spine lights up.

Prey see the light at the end of the spine and swim towards it.

Anglerfish can eat eels and squid that are twice as **big** as themselves.

DEEP-SEA SHARKS

Lots of sharks live in the deep sea.
The cookie-cutter shark is not very
big. It can grow to 50 cm long,
but it has very sharp front teeth.

WOW!
Cookie-cutter
sharks can give
bigger animals
a nasty bite.

The goblin shark eats molluscs, fish and crabs. When the shark senses food nearby, its jaws shoot forward. They snap around the prey and suck it into the shark's mouth.

DEEP-SEA SQUID

Many squid live in the deep sea, 300 m below the surface. The **biggest** squid of all is the colossal squid. It can be longer than a bus!

WOW!

Deep-sea squid have **big** eyes. They help the squid find food in the deep, dark ocean.

Squid *grab* their prey
with their **l o n g** armlike
tentacles. They eat fish, crabs
and shrimp.

GLASS SPONGE

These animals live at the bottom of the sea.
They are called glass sponges because their
spikes are made of the same material as glass.
They fix onto rocks on the seabed and each other.

Glass sponges eat tiny
creatures that float
in the water
around them.

A sea cucumber does not have a shell or bones. Its body is full of liquid. This helps the animal move around.

SEA CUCUMBER

The sea cucumber feeds on tiny plants and animals, and scraps from the seabed. It can bury itself in the sandy sea floor.

SPERM WHALE

These **huge** whales can grow to 18 m long. They can dive down 1,000 m to look for food. A sperm whale can eat 1.36 tonnes of food in a day!

Whales breathe through a blowhole in their head.

Sperm whales have the **biggest** brain of any animal. They live in groups called pods.

GULPER EEL

These long, black eels live deep down in cold, dark water. A gulper eel has a **huge** mouth that opens very wide. It can eat animals as big as itself!

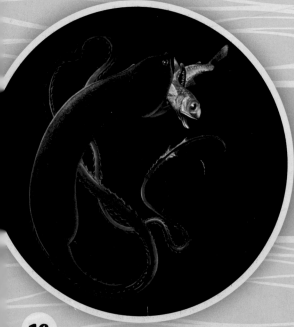

The gulper eel eats fish that swim towards the light on the end of the eel's tail.

This eel has a very **l o n g** tail that helps it move through the water.

CUTTLEFISH

A cuttlefish has eight arms and two tentacles. There are suckers on all of them. The tentacles **grab** prey and pull it towards the cuttlefish's mouth.

WOW!

If a cuttlefish spots a predator, it can let out a cloud of **black ink** and hide in it.

Cuttlefish can change
colour to blend in
with the background.
This helps them catch
fish, crabs and shrimp.

TRIPOD FISH

A tripod fish is just 36 cm long.

But its three stiff fins can be 1 m long.

The fish sits on the fins at the bottom
of the sea and waits for prey to drift by.

WOW!

This fish is also
called a stilt walker
because of the
way it moves.

Hatchetfish have **big**, glowing eyes. They help the fish see food that falls from above.

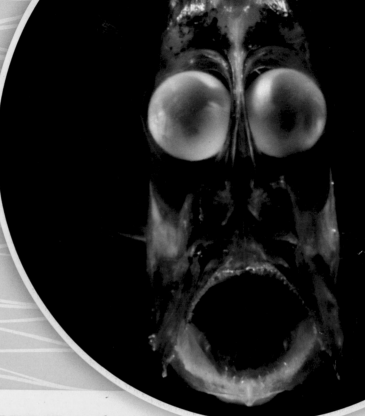

HATCHETFISH

This fish is named for the shape of its body. It is very thin and looks like the blade of a hatchet. Hatchetfish make their own light in the deep, dark sea.

DEEP SEA FACTS

 The deepest seabed is called Challenger Deep. It is in the Pacific Ocean. It is nearly 11 km deep.

 Most deep sea fish have very big eyes. The eyes help them use every bit of light.

 The longest mountain range in the world is underwater. It is called the Mid-Oceanic Ridge. It is more than 56,000 km long.

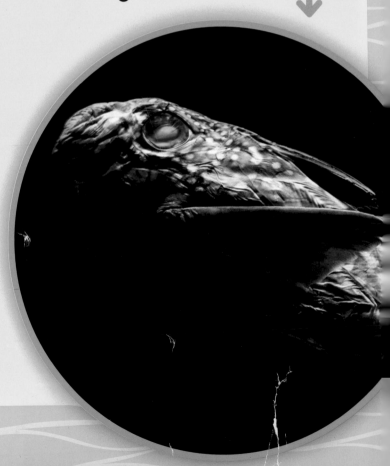

USEFUL WORDS

mollusc
An animal with a soft body.
Most molluscs have a hard shell.
A snail is a mollusc.

predator
An animal that hunts and
kills other animals for food.
Cuttlefish are predators. →

prey
An animal hunted and eaten by another
animal. Fish are the prey of cuttlefish.

trench
A deep underwater ditch.

FIND OUT MORE

First Animal Encyclopedia: Seas and Oceans, Anna Claybourne, Bloomsbury, 2014.

Under the Sea, Anna Milbourne, Usborne, 2012.

The Usborne Big Book of Big Sea Creatures, Minna Lacey, Usborne, 2011.

Visual Explorers: Ocean Life, Paul Calver and Toby Reynolds, Franklin Watts, 2015.

INDEX